16.85

Withdrawn

TRAIN SONG

by Diane Siebert
paintings by Mike Wimmer

HarperCollinsPublishers

Train Song
Text copyright © 1981 by Diane Siebert
Illustrations copyright © 1990 by Michael L. Wimmer
The poem "Train Song" was first published in *Cricket* magazine in 1981.
Printed in Hong Kong. All rights reserved.
Typography by Al Cetta

Library of Congress Cataloging-in-Publication Data
Siebert, Diane.
    Train song / by Diane Siebert ; illustrated by Mike Wimmer. — 1st ed.
        p.   cm.
    Summary: Rhymed text and illustrations describe the journeys of a
variety of transcontinental trains.
    ISBN 0-690-04726-6. — ISBN 0-690-04728-2 (lib. bdg.)
    ISBN 0-06-443340-4 (pbk.)
    [1. Railroads—Trains—Fiction.   2. Stories in rhyme.]   I. Wimmer,
Mike, ill.   II. Title.
PZ8.3.S5725Tp   1990   88-389
[E]—dc19   CIP
                                                            AC

TRAIN SONG

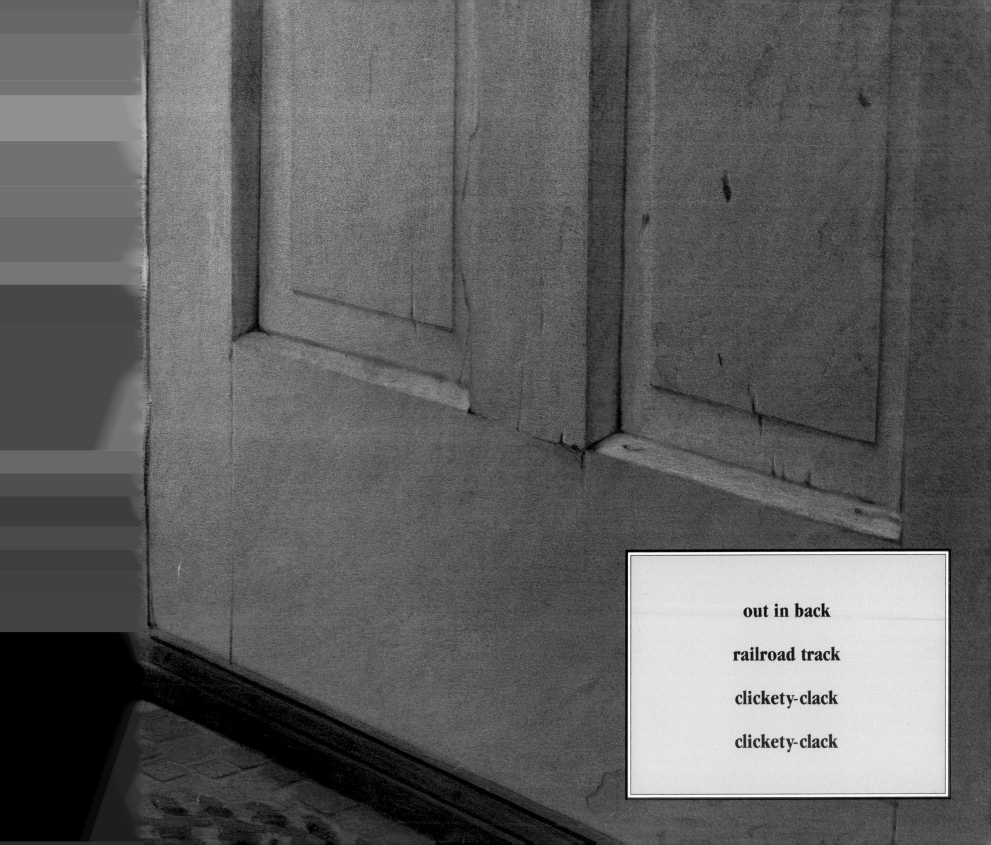

out in back

railroad track

clickety-clack

clickety-clack

locomotives

cars in tow

going places:

Buffalo

New York City

Boston, Mass.

slowing 'neath the overpass

Dallas

Fort Worth

Abilene

with stops at all points

in between

steel wheels rolling

on steel trails

rumbling

grumbling

on steel rails

engineers with striped hats

head-of-the-line aristocrats

up in front

sitting high

see them wave as they go by

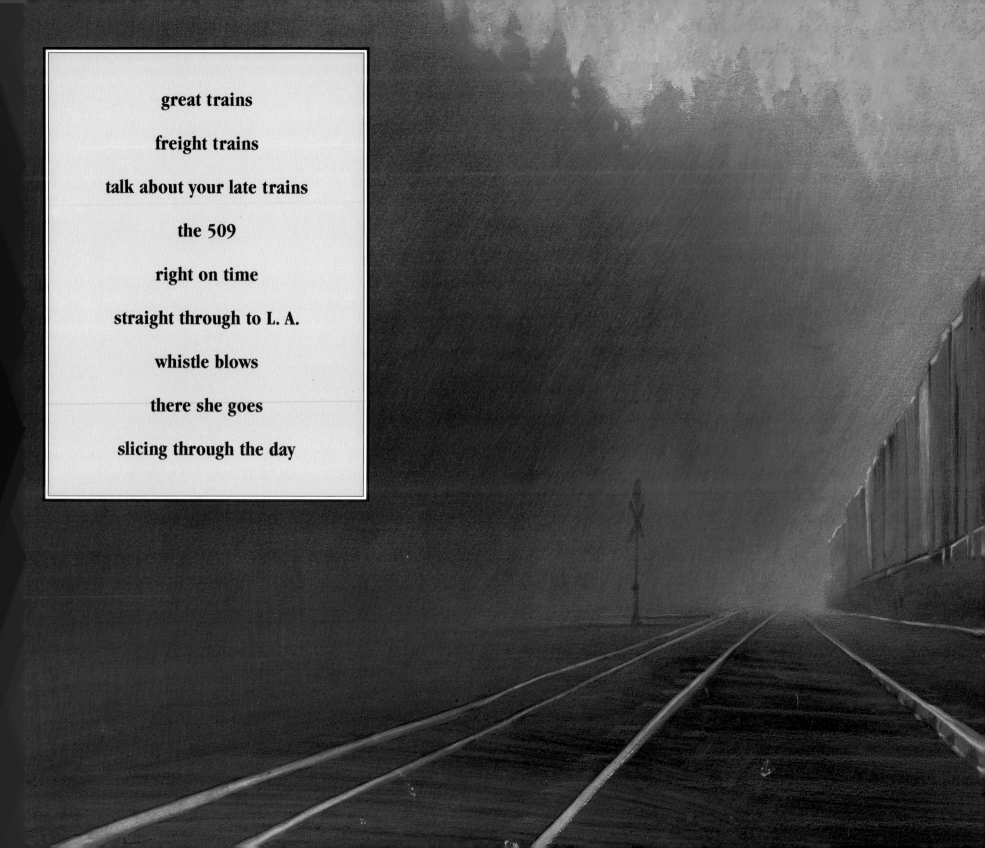

great trains

freight trains

talk about your late trains

the 509

right on time

straight through to L. A.

whistle blows

there she goes

slicing through the day

boxcars

flatcars

going-to-North Platte cars:

Cotton Belt

Santa Fe

New York Central

on their way

long trains

strong trains

singing-clickety-song trains

cars with lumber

cars with cattle

clickety-clacking

to Seattle

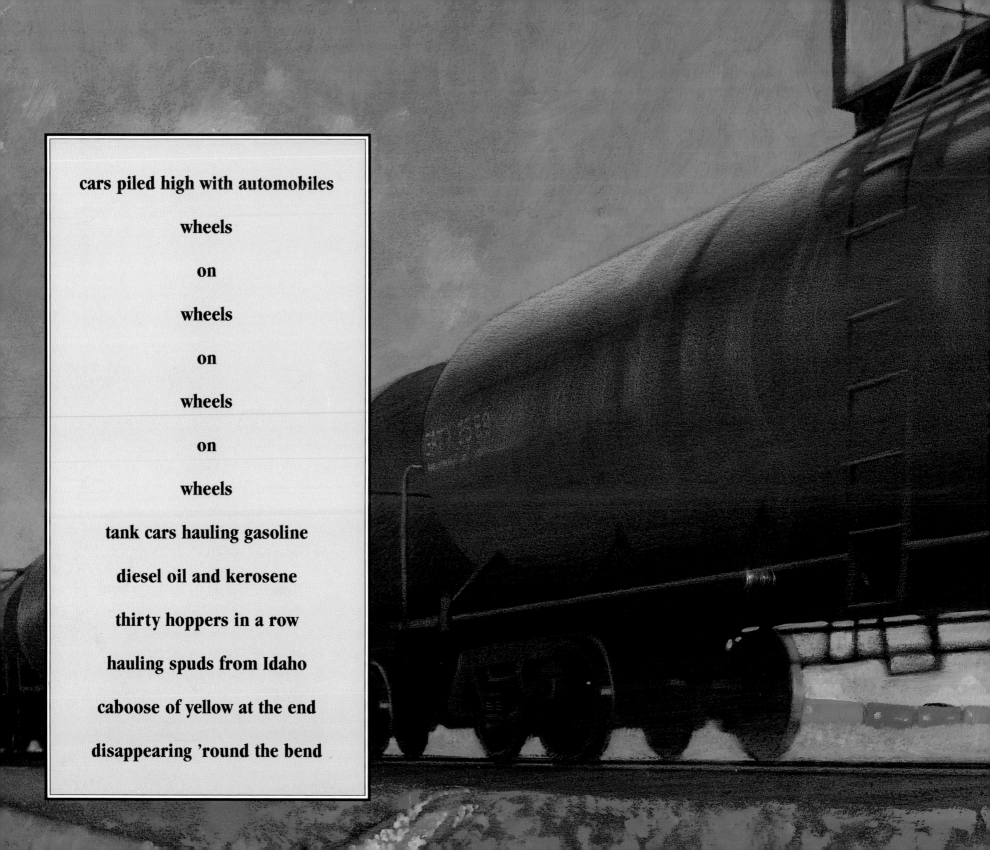

cars piled high with automobiles

wheels

on

wheels

on

wheels

on

wheels

tank cars hauling gasoline

diesel oil and kerosene

thirty hoppers in a row

hauling spuds from Idaho

caboose of yellow at the end

disappearing 'round the bend

trains with passengers on board

clickety-clacking

rolling toward

their destinations far away

clickety-clacking

night and day

coaches

club cars

diners, too

dome cars with a perfect view

signal lights

green

yellow

red

railroad station up ahead

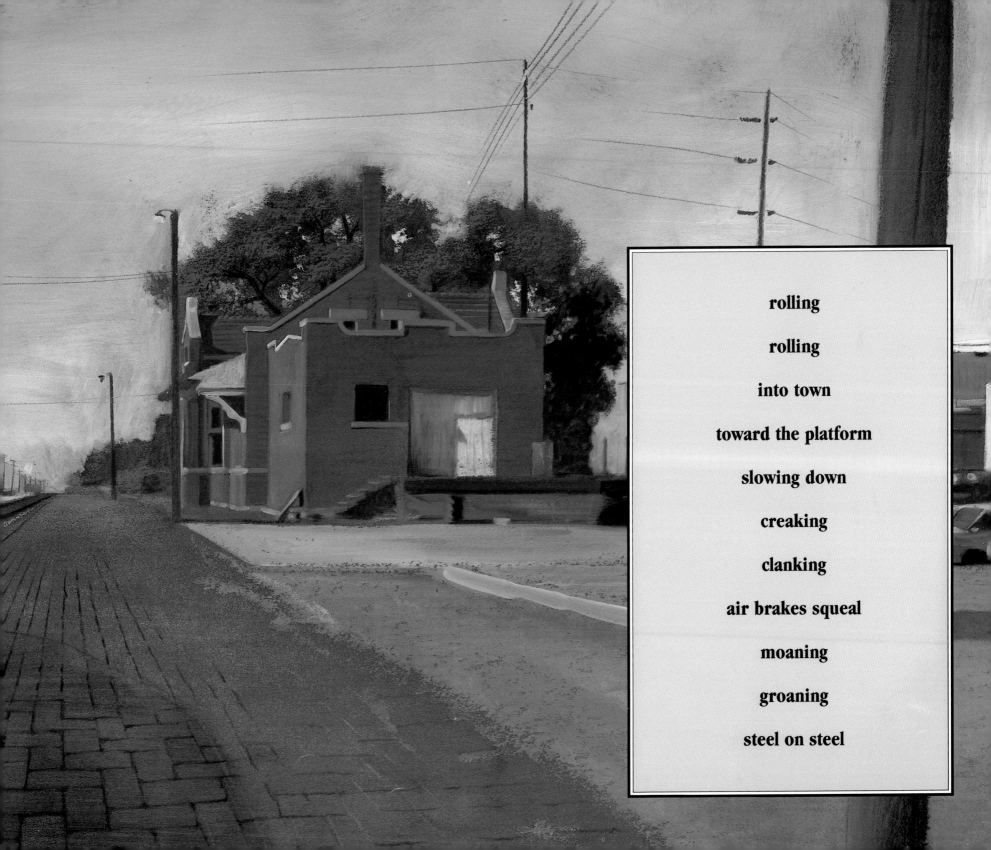

rolling

rolling

into town

toward the platform

slowing down

creaking

clanking

air brakes squeal

moaning

groaning

steel on steel

PASSENGER TRAIN SCHEDULE

TRACK	TRAIN NAME	DEPARTS	ARRIVES
4	Walla Walla	2:30p	9:30a
8	BAY AREA SLEEPER	8:00p	12:00p
3	Daylight	4:30	3

Overnighter to the bay

arrive at noon on Saturday

get a sleeper

don't be late

she's waiting on Track number 8

head conductor

dressed in black

peering up and down the track

checks his watch

now hear him shout:

"ALL ABOARD"

she's pulling out!

through the tunnel

going fast

clickety-clack

she's roaring past

the cities, suburbs, little towns

past forest greens and desert browns

spikes and crossties

smooth, worn rails

through the twilight

whistle wails

feel the rhythm

hear the sound

clickety-clacking

homeward bound

say good night

and

wave good-bye

hear the railroad lullaby